T0392300

The secret
of
Chinese Cooking

MEIRU LUDLOW

AuthorHouse™ UK
1663 Liberty Drive
Bloomington, IN 47403 USA
www.authorhouse.co.uk
Phone: 0800 047 8203 (Domestic TFN)
+44 1908 723714 (International)

Published by AuthorHouse 06/29/2019

ISBN: 978-1-7283-9024-6 (sc)
ISBN: 978-1-7283-9023-9 (e)

Print information available on the last page.

This book is printed on acid-free paper.

authorHOUSE®

CONTENTS

ABOUT THIS BOOK

I hope this book is an easy to use guide for anybody who enjoys Chinese food and wants to cook Chinese food from fresh.

In this book, I separate Chinese cooking into two parts. One part is the quick and easy to cook dishes, another part is more traditional Chinese dishes. In the end, I listed the commonly used cooking sauces and cooking methods.

Cooking Chinese food is easy. You can replace any ingredients in a recipe to create your favourite dishes. If you are a vegetarian, you can remove the meat in a recipe to make it suitable for you. That's why there are countless varieties in Chinese cuisine.

To master the skill of cooking Chinese food, you need to understand the cooking methods and how to create a flavour. By combining sauces and cooking methods you will be able to create your own favourite dishes.

The recipes in this book are used at my Cooking Classes. They are the most popular dishes loved by my learners. All of my learners were required to create one or two dishes by themselves after a five-week course. They all did very well. I believe you can too. Let choose a recipe and start cooking………

QUICK AND EASY
TO COOK DISHES

VEGETABLE AND SEAFOOD

Green tea flavoured king prawns

Ingredients:

- 200 gm raw King Prawns,
- 50 gm carrot,
- 50 gm mangetout,
- 1 spring onion finely chopped,
- 1 Tea Spoon finely chopped ginger,
- 1 Table Spoon Chinese Yellow Rice Wine,
- 1 Tea Spoon salt,
- ¼ Tea Spoon sugar,
- 1 Tea Spoon corn starch,
- A Table Spoon Green Tea leaves +1/4 cup boiling water,
- a few drops of veg oil

Cooking Method:

1. Peel the skin of king prawns. Slice the back of king prawns open (or slice the king prawns in halves) to take the black line out.
2. Soak the tea leaves in a ¼ cup of just boiled water, covered with a lid.
3. Marinate the prawns in Yellow Rice Wine and salt.
4. Slice the carrot into thin slices.
5. Cut each mangetout into halves.
6. When the green tea has cool down, pour the tea out into a small bowl, and then, mix the cornflour with the green tea.
7. Heat up a few drops of vegetable oil in a wok, when it is medium hot, stir fry the king prawns for 4 minutes or when the raw king prawns become pink, put the king prawns in a dish to use later. Re-heat up the wok with some oil, put ginger and spring onion in sauté to bring out fragrance, after that, add carrot and mangetout in to sauté for 1-2 minutes until they are lightly cooked, sprinkle some salt and sugar, add the cooked king prawn and the green tea and cornflour mixture, toss to mix everything together well, and then, transferring everything to a plate to serve immediately.

Stir-fried seasonal vegetables in garlic sauce

Ingredients

- 70 gm baby corn,
- 100 gm mushroom,
- ½ red pepper,
- 2 garlic cloves,

- 1 spring onion
- ½ tea spoon salt,
- 1 tea spoon corn starch.
- Some vegetable oil for stir-frying.

Cooking Method

1. Slice one baby corn to 2 or 3 pieces.
2. Slice one mushroom to 4 pieces.
3. Slice the red pepper to diagonal shape approx. 1.5 cm X 1.5cm.
4. Slice the spring onion to small pieces and chop the garlic cloves to mince.
5. Mix the corn starch with 50ml cold water in a small bowl.
6. Heat up some vegetable oil in a wok on high heat. When the oil is hot, put the spring onion pieces in, toss to bring out the fragrance. After that, add the baby corns, mushrooms and pepper into stirfry for a couple of minutes, and then, add the minced garlic in, toss to mix everything well. Pouring the corn starch mixture genteelly around the wall of the wok. Stirfry to cover everything in the thickened sauce. Transfer them to a dish to serve immediately.

Stir-fried Potato and Tomato

It is quick and easy to cook. And it goes well with rice. It is also suitable for vegans and vegetarians.

Ingredients

- 200 gm canned tomatoes,
- 1 Table Spoon Tomato Puree
- 1 baking potato,
- 1 spring onion,
- 1 garlic clove, finely chopped.

- ½ Tea Spoon salt,
- 1 Tea Spoon sugar,
- 1 chilli slice into small pieces,
- A few drops of vegetable oil.
- Approx. 1 Table Spoon coriander to garnish.

Cooking method,

1. Peel the potato, and then slice it to thin strips, approx. 0.2 cm or 0.1" thin. Soak in a bowl of cold water for 10 minutes.
2. Slice Spring onion to small pieces and garlic to fine piece.
3. Heat up a few drops of vegetable oil (approx. 1 Table Spoon) in a wok on high heat. When the oil is semi-hot, put spring onion pieces in, sauté for a minute, add potato strips and tomato puree in toss to mix them well, and then, add the tomato and chilli pieces. Sauté to mix and cook everything for a couple of minutes, and then, add the salt and sugar, in the end, add the garlic pieces, mix them in and transfer them to a dish, sprinkle the coriander pieces to garnish, serve immediately.

Country Style Pancakes

Ingredients:

- ½ cup of sweet corn,
- ½ cup of plain flour,
- ¼ cup of sliced Chinese wild mushrooms or Chestnut mushrooms (0.5 X 0.5 cm size pieces),
- 200 gm spinach
- ½ cup of water,

- ¼ cup of finely chopped spring onion,
- 2 Table Spoon finely chopped Sichuan Pickle,
- ½ Tea Spoon salt (optional),
- 1 Tea Spoon Chinese Five Spices,
- ½ cup of vegetable oil for cooking.

Cooking methods:

1. Heat up a wok. When it is hot, put the spinach in to cook. When the spinach is soft, turned the heat off and wait until the spinach has cool down. Take the spinach out and slice the spinach to smaller pieces.
2. Mix all the ingredients together except vegetable oil to make a pancake mixture.
3. Heat up some vegetable oil in a frying pan. When the oil is medium hot, put ¼ cup of mixture in the frying pan to cook for 2-3 minutes, and then flip over to cook another side for 2-3 minutes.
4. Repeat the process until using up all the pancake mixture.
5. Put them in a plate to serve immediately.

Stir-fried Green Pokchoi and chestnut mushrooms in Oyster sauce

Ingredients:

- 2 Chinese green Pckchois,
- 5 - 6 chestnut mushrooms
- 1 Table Spoon oyster sauce,
- ¼ Tea Spoon Salt;
- ½ Tea Spoon white pepper,
- ½ Tea Spoon sugar,

- A couple of slices of ginger, chopped into fine pieces,
- 1 spring onion finely chopped,
- 1 Garlic clove finely chopped,
- 1 Tea Spoon corn starch + 1 Table Spoon tap water, mixed.
- 1 Table Spoon vegetable oil.

Cooking Methods:

1. Sliced the Pakchoi to 4 – 5 cm (or approx. 2 inches) length.
2. Heat up 1 Table Spoon oil on high heat, when oil is hot, put spring onion and ginger pieces in to stir fry for a few seconds,
3. Add Pckchois in, stir fry for another minute; add Chestnuts mushrooms, Oyster sauce, White Pepper, and Sugar. Keep tossing for a couple of minutes until everything is mixed well.
4. Pouring the corn starch mixture around the wall of the wok, add garlic pieces in, toss to coat everything in the thickened sauce, and then, transfer them to a plate to serve immediately.

Hot and Sour soup

Ingredients:

- 350 ml cold water + 1 Tea Spoon chicken flavour powder;
- ½ Tea Spoon White pepper or to taste;
- ¼ cup of sliced bamboo shoots strips;
- ¼ cup of sliced Muer (a type of Chinese mushroom. It's thin and dark brown colour.);
- ¼ cup of sliced fresh bean curd strips;
- 1 egg beaten;
- 1 Table Spoon corn starch + 2 Table Spoon water, mix well.
- 1 Table Spoon dark rice vinegar,
- ½ Tea Spoon sugar,
- 1 Tea Spoon sesame seed oil.
- Some sliced coriander or spring onion (optional)

Cooking Methods:

1. Heat up a sauce pan, put the water in. When it is boiling, add the bamboo shoots, Muer and the bean curd in the sauce pan. Cook for 3 minutes in gentle heat. Add the chicken flavour powder in, mix it genteelly, pouring corn-starch mixture genteelly in the soup. Stir slowly while pouring the corn-starch mixture in. when it is boiling, add the beaten egg in the soup slowly in swirl movement; wait for 1 minute until the egg is set.
2. Put the white pepper and the vinegar in a serving bowl.
3. Transfer the soup to the bowl.
4. Sprinkle coriander or spring onion pieces on the soup, after that, sprinkle a few drops of sesame seed oil.
5. Stir the soup genteelly to mix the pepper and the vinegar in and serve immediately.

CHICKEN

Chicken in Black Bean Sauce

Ingredients:

- 1 piece of chicken breast,
- ½ any coloured pepper,
- ½ onion,
- 1 Table Spoon black bean sauce,
- 1 Tea Spoon dark soy sauce,
- ½ Tea Spoon sugar,
- 1 Table Spoon Yellow Rice Wine,
- 1 Tea Spoon ground Sichuan pepper,
- 1 Tea Spoon Corn Starch,
- 1 garlic clove, finely chopped,
- A few drops of vegetable oil.

Cooking Method:

1. Slice the chicken breast into thin slices, approx. 0.2cm or 0.1" thin. And then, marinate the chicken in yellow rice wine and ground Sichuan pepper in a small bowl.
2. Slice the Pepper, and the onion to about 2.5cm X 2.5 cm or 1" X 1" pieces to match with the chicken.
3. Heat up a few drops of vegetable oil in a wok. Put approx. 1 Tea Spoon corn starch to coat marinated chicken evenly. When the oil is hot, put the chicken pieces into cook for about 5 minutes or until the chicken is cooked. After that, put the cooked chicken pieces in a dish to use later.
4. Heat up some vegetable oil in the wok again. When the oil is semi-hot, put the onion pieces in, sauté, and then, add the pepper in, toss to mix everything well, put the chicken back, toss again, add 1 Table Spoon black bean sauce, 1 tea spoon dark soy sauce and the sugar in, toss to mix everything well. In the end, put the garlic pieces in, toss to mix them well, and then, transfer them to a plate to serve immediately.

Fish Fragrant Chicken Strips

Ingredients:

- 1 piece of chicken breast, about 150gm -170gm;
- ½ pepper, preferable green coloured pepper;
- 1 small carrot about 70 gm;
- 2 dry chillis; or 1 Tea Spoon (tea spoon) Sichuan chilli paste

- 1 Table Spoon finely sliced ginger;
- 1 Table Spoon finely sliced spring onion;
- 1 Table Spoon finely sliced garlic;
- 1 Table Spoon tomato puree;
- 1 Table Spoon vegetable oil.

Mix the following ingredients together in a small bowl.

- 1 Table Spoon sugar;
- 1 Table Spoon white rice vinegar;
- 2 Table Spoon yellow rice wine;
- 1 Tea Spoon (tea spoon) light soy sauce;

- 1 Tea Spoon (tea spoon) dark soy sauce;
- 1 Table Spoon corn starch
- 4 Table Spoon cold water, mix well.

Cooking Method:

1. Slice the chicken breast into thin strips, approx. 2-3 mm thin X 40 – 50 mm long. And then, sprinkle some salt and pour 1 Table Spoon yellow rice wine over the chicken strips to marinate.
2. Slice the green pepper, carrot, ginger, Spring onion, garlic and chilli to the similar size strips;
3. Mix the sugar, white rice vinegar, yellow rice wine, dark soy sauce, light soy sauce, corn flour and cold water together in a small bowl.
4. Heat up some vegetable oil in a wok, when oil is hot, put chicken strips in, stir fry for about 10 minutes or until they are cooked. Transfer cooked chicken strips to a plate to use later.
5. Re-heat the wok, put tomato puree in to sauté, and then, add sliced carrot and pepper in the wok, sauté for a few minutes, add sliced ginger, garlic, and spring onion in, after that, add the chilli in, in the end, put the cooked chicken strips back to the wok, toss to mix everything well, pouring the sauce mixture gradually to the wok, toss to mix everything well, and then transfer it to a plate to serve immediately.

Gongbao / Kung po Chicken

Ingredients:

- 300 gm Chicken leg meat skinless and boneless;
- 1 Table Spoon light soy sauce,
- 1 Table Spoon Shao Xing Rice Wine,
- 1 Tea Spoon (tea spoon) ground Sichuan pepper,
- 1 Table Spoon Corn flour.
- ½ green pepper,
- ½ cup of cooked peanuts,

- A few dry chilis adjust to suit your taste.
- 1 Table Spoon cooking oil, such as vegetable oil, peanut oil, sunflower oil, etc.
- 3 or 4 pieces of ginger at 1mm thick, 2 garlic cloves sliced to 1mm thick, 4 spring onions slice to 30mm long.

Mix the following ingredients together to make a sauce mixture.

- *1 Table Spoon white sugar,*
- *1 Table Spoon dark rice vinegar,*
- *2 Table Spoon light soy sauce,*

- *1 Table Spoon Shao Xing Rice Wine,*
- *1 Table Spoon Corn flour,*
- *4 Table Spoon cold water*

Cooking Method:

1. Slice the chicken meat to approx. 1.5 cm cube pieces, and then, marinate them in 1Table Spoon light soy sauce, 1Table Spoon Shao Xing Rice Wine, 1Tea Spoon ground Sichuan pepper and 1Table Spoon corn flour for 1 hour if possible;
2. Slice the green pepper to the similar size pieces;
3. Mix the white sugar, dark rice vinegar, light soy sauce, Shao Xing Rice wine and corn flour together in a mixing bowl.
4. Heat up a wok on medium heat, when the oil is semi-hot, put chicken pieces in one by one, slowly fry the chicken pieces for approx. 10 minutes until golden brown. Turn off the heat and transfer the chicken pieces to a dish.
5. Heat up a wok with 1 Table Spoon cooking oil on high heat. When the oil is hot, put the garlic, ginger, and spring onion pieces in, sauté to bring out the fragrance, put the green pepper pieces in, toss to mix them together, and then, add the cooked chicken and the chili pieces in, keep moving them in the wok while pouring the sauce mixture in gradually. When everything is covered in the sauce, add the peanuts, toss to mix peanuts in, and then, transfer them to a dish to serve immediately.

Chicken cashew nuts in Yellow bean sauce

Ingredients:

- 1 piece of chicken breast,
- 1 Tea Spoon Five-spices
- ¼ Tea Spoon salt + ¼ Tea Spoon salt,
- 1 Table Spoon Yellow Rice Wine,
- 50 gm roasted cashew nuts,

- 1 spring onion,
- 1 Table Spoon Yellow Bean Sauce,
- 1 Tea Spoon Sugar,
- A few drops of vegetable oil.

Cooking Method:

1. Slice the chicken breast into big strips, approx. 2 cm cubes thick,
2. Marinate the chicken breast in salt, yellow rice wine and Five-spices,
3. Slice the spring onion into small pieces,
4. Heat up a wok with a few drops of veg oil. When the oil is semi-hot, put the chicken in, stir fry for 5 minutes until chicken is cooked thoroughly. Put spring onion pieces in, saute until smell the fragrance, add yellow bean sauce and sugar, stir fry everything well, in the end, add the cashew nuts in, toss to mix everything well (sprinkle some finely chopped spring onion to garnish optional) and transfer them to a dish to serve immediately.

Crispy Sweet and Sour Chicken

Ingredients:

Batter mixture:

- ½ cup of Plain Flour,
- ¼ cup of Corn Flour,
- ½ Tea Spoon Baking Powder,
- ½ Tea Spoon Bicarbonate of Soda,
- 180 ml cold water.

Mix well above ingredients together in a mixing bowl, and then, leave it in the fridge for minimum of 2 hours to rest.

- 1 piece of chicken breast, 150 gm.
- ½ white onion,
- ½ Green pepper & ½ Red pepper;
- 1 Table Spoon veg oil,
- ½ Tea Spoon chicken flavour powder,
- 1 Tea Spoon salt,
- 2 Table Spoon clear rice vinegar,
- 2 Table Spoon sugar,
- 2 Table Spoon ketchup,
- 1 Table Spoon corn starch,
- 3 Table Spoon cold water.
- 2 Cups of Vegetable Oil.

Cooking Method:

1. Slice chicken breast into approx. 3 cm X 3cm X 0.4 cm thick pieces and then marinate in 1 Table Spoon yellow rice wine.
2. Slice white onion and pepper into similar size pieces.
3. Mix White Rice Vinegar, Sugar, Ketchup, Corn Starch, and water together in a small mixing bowl.
4. Heat up the vegetable oil in a wok. When the oil is semi-hot, put battered chicken pieces in, cook for about 5 minutes until they are golden brown colour. And then, put them in a dish to use later. (Please note, fry the chicken pieces one by one, give them enough space in the oil, and do not put them in altogether.)
5. Heat up a few drops of vegetable oil in a wok. When oil is very hot, put onion pieces in, stir fry for 1 minute, add pepper, stir fry for another minute, add salt and chicken flavour powder in, and then add ingredient mixture in around the side of wok, keep stir frying until sauce is thickened, then, add fried chicken pieces in. Mix everything well, coat sauce on chicken pieces, after that transfer them in a dish to serve immediately.

PORK

Cantonese Roast Pork / Char Siu Pork

Main ingredient

Port Shoulder meat approx 500 gm,

Ingredients for Marinade:

- 1 Tea Spoon Dark Soy Sauce,
- 5 Table Spoon Light Soy Sauce,
- 2 Table Spoon Yellow Rice Wine,
- 1 Table Spoon Hoisin Sauce,
- 4 Table Spoon Clear Honey
- 1 Tea Spoon Red Yeast Rice Powder (optional) or Red food colouring.

Method of Marinating Pork

1. Mix the ingredients for marinade altogether in a mixing bowl or a container,
2. Put the pork in the marinade. Marinating for a minimum of 8 hours, for best result overnight.

Cooking method

1. Preheat an oven to gas mark 2, (300 F / 150 C). Putting about 1 pint of tap water in the baking tray about 0.8 – 1.0 cm deep. Water should cover the bottom.
2. Put a wire rack in the baking tray, it should be above the water and with some space in between.
3. Put the pork on the rack, cook in the oven for 1½ hours. And then, turn up the heat to Gas mark 4, (350F / 180C) to cook for 30 minutes. Brush the marinate on the pork regularly while cooking to give the meat a glossy looking.
4. When it is cooked, turn the heat off to let the pork rest for about 10 minutes, they can be served straight away on its own, example, slice to some pieces to serve as a starter, or use them to make sandwiches, wraps or salad, etc.

Char Siu Pork crispy noodles

Ingredients

- 200 gm fresh noodles or dry noodles,
- 250 gm Char Siu Pork, freshly cooked in an oven,
- 4 spring onions, slice into smaller pieces approx. 5mm length,
- 100 gm mushrooms, slice into smaller pieces,
- 60 gm baby corns, slice into smaller pieces,
- ½ green pepper,
- 1 Table Spoon finely chopped garlic,
- 1 Table Spoon Oyster sauce,
- 1 Table Spoon Yellow rice wine,
- 1 Tea Spoon white sugar,
- 1 Table Spoon corn starch or corn flour mixed in a ¼ cup of cold water.
- 2 cups of vegetable oil.

Method of preparing noodles

1. Using 2mm diameter fresh noodles -- Heat up some water in a pot or pan. When water is boiling, put noodles in, boiling for 2-5 minutes or until the noodle is soft. Drain the water, leave the noodles aside to use later.
2. Using 1mm diameter dry noodles – Soak the noodles in scalding hot water for a few minutes until noodle is soft.
3. Using 2mm diameter fresh noodles without precooking.

Cooking Method

1. Heat up a frying pan on medium heat, when oil is hot sliding prepared noodles into fry for about 5-8 minutes or until noodles are crispy. Put the noodles in a plate.
2. At the same time of frying noodles, heat up a wok with 1 Table Spoon vegetable oil. When oil is hot, put some spring onion pieces in, sauté to bring out fragrant, add Oyster sauce, white sugar, yellow rice wine and garlic pieces, sauté to mix them well, and then, add mushroom, baby corn and green pepper in, toss to cover the vegetable in the sauce, after that, pouring the corn starch mixture around the wall of the wok to thicken the sauce. Once the sauce is thickened, transfer them onto the top of fried noodles.
3. Arranging sliced Char Siu Pork on the top of the dish, sprinkle the rest of spring onion pieces on the top to garnish the dish.
4. Enjoy!

French beans with meatballs

Ingredients:

- 250 gm pork mince,
- A ¼ cup of bread crumbs
- 1 spring onions finely chopped
- 1 Table spoon of finely chopped ginger
- 1 egg beaten
- 1 Table Spoon Sesame seed oil
- 1 Table Spoon Light soy sauce

- 1 Table Spoon Dark soy sauce
- Some salt to your taste
- 1 Tea Spoon chicken flavour powder mix in ¼ cup scalding hot water.
- Some vegetable oil
- 100 gm French beans slice into smaller pieces.
- 2 Garlic cloves finely chopped

Ingredients required to make the sauce:

- ½ Tea Spoon chicken flavour power
- 1 Tea Spoon dark soy sauce

- ½ cup of cold water
- 1 Tea Spoon corn flour + a little water to mix

Cooking method:

1. In a mixing bowl, mix the pork mince, spring onion pieces, ginger, egg, sesame seed oil, light soy sauce and dark soy sauce together, and then, add bread crumbs and chicken flavour mixture. Keep mixing until it becomes a paste.
2. Heat up a wok with approx. 2 Table Spoon vegetable oil. Using a spoon to shape meatballs. When the oil is warm, start to put meatballs in. Leave the meatballs in the wok to fry for a few minutes until they are firm, and then, turn them genteelly to cook other sides. Once they are cooked, put them in a dish to use later.
3. Put the French beans in the wok and sauté for a minute. Add dark soy sauce, chicken flavour powder and cold water in the wok, and then, put meatballs back to the wok. Cook on high heat for about 5 minutes, and then, add the garlic pieces in, after that,pour the corn starch in slowly and moving the wok genteelly to thicken the sauce. When the sauce is thickened, transfer them to a plate to enjoy immediately.

Mangetout stir-fried with bacon

Ingredient:

- 100 gm mangetout,
- 1 Tea Spoon vegetable oil.
- 1 spring onion,
- 3 slices of bacon (thick sliced is preferred),
- 1 Tea Spoon corn starch + 1 Table Spoon tap water.

Cooking Method

1. Slice bacon into 1-inch wide piece; slice spring onion into fine pieces.
2. Mix corn starch with water.
3. Heat up a wok with 1 Tea Spoon veg oil, when oil is hot, put bacon pieces in, stir fry for 1 – 2 minutes, add Mangetout in, stir fry for 1 minute, sprinkle spring onion pieces in, pour corn starch mixture in, stir fry to mix everything well, transfer them to a dish to serve immediately.

Hongshao Pork

Ingredients:

- 500 gm pork belly, sliced to approx. 4 cm or (1.5")long;
- 1 Table Spoon vegetable oil,
- 2 Table Spoon Hoi Sin sauce,
- 1 Table Spoon Dark Soy Sauce,
- 1 - ½ cup cold water,
- 1 Table Spoon Chinese Crystal sugar,
- 1 or 2 Spring onions,
- 2 Garlic Cloves, finely chopped;
- 1 Tea Spoon Chinese Five Spices,
- 1 Tea Spoon Red Colouring rice powder,
- 1 Table Spoon Yellow Rice Wine
- 4 spring onions
- 5 gm ginger, slice into 3 mm thick pieces

Cooking Method:

1. Heat up 1 pint of water in a sauce pan, add pork pieces, ginger, spring onion and yellow rice wine in. Boiling for 10 minutes. Washing the pork pieces with hot water, and then, put aside to use later.
2. Mix the Hoisin sauce, Dark Soy Sauce, water, Chinese Crystal sugar, Chinese Five Spices, Food colouring rice powder, and Yellow Rice wine together in a mixing bowl.
3. Heat up a wok with some vegetable oil. When the oil is semi-hot, put spring onion pieces and minced garlic in, sauté to bring the fragrant, and then add the pork pieces in, sauté for a few minutes, add the mixed sauces in, bring the sauce to boiling. When it is boiling, turn the heat down to shimmer for 40 minutes or until the meat is soft and tender. Turn the heat up to thicken the sauce. When the sauce is thickened and looks sticky, transfer the pork to a dish to serve immediately.

Hongshao Mini Ribs

Ingredients:

- 500 gm meaty mini ribs approx. 4 cm or (1.5") long;
- A few drops of vegetable oil,
- 2 Table Spoon Hoi Sin sauce,
- 1 Table Spoon Light Soy Sauce,
- ¼ cup broth,
- 1 ½ Table Spoon Chinese Crystal sugar,
- 1 or 2 Spring onions,
- 2 Garlic Cloves, finely chopped;
- 1 Tea Spoon Chinese Five Spices,
- 1 Tea Spoon Red colouring rice powder,
- 1 Table Spoon Yellow Rice Wine

Cooking Method:

1. Heat up a sauce pan with 1 pint of tap water, put the ribs in and boiling for 45 minutes or 1 hour until the meat is soft.
2. Mix the Hoisin sauce, Light Soy Sauce, water, Chinese Crystal sugar, Chinese Five Spices, red colouring rice, and Yellow Rice wine together.
3. Heat up a wok with a few drops of vegetable oil. When the oil is semi-hot, put garlic and spring onion pieces in, and then the mixed sauce, bring the sauce to boiling. Add the mini ribs in, put a lid on the wok, and then let it simmer for 10 - 20 minutes. When the sauce is getting thicker, genteelly turn the ribs another side to make sure they are covered in the sauce. (Sprinkle some sesame seeds to decorate, optional) After that, transfer the ribs to a dish to serve immediately.

Yuxiang Aubergine Pot

Yu Xiang (Fish Fragrant) Aubergine Pot,

Ingredients:

- 1 Aubergine,
- 100 gm Pork mince,
- 1 TSP yellow rice wine,
- 2 Spring onions,
- 2 slices fresh ginger,
- 2 garlic cloves,
- ½ TBSP Chilli paste,
- 1 TBSP tomato puree,

- 250 ml cold water + ½ TSP chicken flavour mixed together,
- 1 TBSP light soy sauce,
- ½ TSP Dark soy sauce,
- 1 TSP Dark Rice Vinegar,
- 1 TSP Sugar,
- 3 TSP corn starch + 3 TBSP cold water to mix
- Some vegetable oil to cook.

Cooking method,

1. Slice the aubergine into thick strips, approx. 1.3 cm X 1.3 cm or 0.5" X 0.5" thick.
2. Shred the garlic, ginger into fine pieces, and spring onion into small pieces.
3. Marinate pork mince in the yellow rice wine,
4. Mixing the light soy sauce, dark soy sauce, dark rice vinegar, sugar and some spring onion and ginger pieces together in a small mixing bowl,
5. Heat up some oil in a wok or a frying pan, when oil is semi-hot, put aubergine strips in to cook side by side until they are soft and light brown. Put cooked aubergine strips in a dish to use later.
6. Heat up some oil in a wok, add spring onion, garlic and ginger in the wok to stir fry until fragrant smell comes out, and then, add pork mince in to. When pork mine is almost cooked, add tomato puree and chilli paste in, mix everything well, and then, add the mixed sauce in and the prepared water in bringing to boiling. When it is boiling, mix the cooked aubergine in, and then sprinkle corn-starch mixture to thicken the sauce.
7. Transfer the dish to a casserole pot or a heatproof dish; simmer on a gentle heat until gravy is near absorbed.
8. Turn the heat off, sprinkle fresh garlic and spring onion pieces on the top, and mix slightly before serving.

Tianjin Style Aubergine

Ingredients:

- 1 or 2 Aubergine,
- 100 gm pork mince,
- 1 Table spoon Beijing roast duck sauce / sweet bean sauce,
- A pinch of salt,
- ¼ cup of chopped coriander,
- 2 garlic cloves finely chopped,
- 2 Table spoon vegetable oil.
- 1 Spring onion sliced to fine pieces(optional)

Cooking Method:

1. Slice the aubergine to 1cm tubes.
2. Heat up a wok with some vegetable oil. When the oil is hot, put the diced aubergine in and cook the aubergine until it is a golden-brown colour. Put the aubergine on a plate to use later.
3. Heat up the wok again with a little bit of oil, when the oil is hot, add the pork mince. Sauté to cook the pork mince, and then, add the spring onion pieces and salt. Sauté further until it has a fragrant smell. Add the Beijing roast duck sauce, followed by the cooked aubergine, sauté to mix everything well. Add garlic pieces and coriander pieces before quickly sauté to make sure everything is covered in sauce. Transfer them to a dish to enjoy immediately.

BEEF AND LAMB

Crispy Chilli Beef

Ingredients:

- 200 gm Beef fillet,
- 3 Table Spoon corn flour,
- A pinch of Sichuan Huajiao, and a pinch of salt,
- 1 small white onion,
- ½ Green pepper,
- 2 medium size chillies,
- 1 garlic clove,
- 2 cups of vegetable oil.

- ½ cup cold water,
- ½ Tea Spoon dark soy sauce,
- 1 Table Spoon corn starch,
- 2 Table Spoon sugar,
- 1 Tea Spoon chicken flavour powder,
- 1 Tea Spoon finely chopped chives to garnish, optional.

Cooking Method:

1. Slice the beef fillet to thin strips, approx 0.2 cm X 5 cm (0.1 X 2.5 in). Dust the Sichuan Huajiao and salt on the beef strips.
2. Slice the white onion into thin strips, approx 2 cm (1 in) wide; and slice the pepper into the similar size.
3. Cut the chillies into small pieces. And chop the garlic into fine pieces.
4. Mix the water, dark soy sauce, corn starch, sugar, and chicken flavour powder together, and then, leave it aside to use later.
5. Coat the beef strips in corn flour one by one completely, once it is all done, heat up a wok with the vegetable oil. When the oil is very hot, almost smoking, turn the heat down a bit, and put a few coated beef strips in the oil to fry for 2 minutes. Repeat until finish frying all the beef strips.
6. Heat up a wok or if using the same wok, pour away most of the oil, leaving only about 1 Table Spoon in it, reheat it up, add chilli pieces and garlic in the wok, toss for a few seconds, and add the pepper and the onion in, toss again, add the sauce mixture in. when the sauce is boiling, add the fried beef strips in. Toss to coat sauce on the beef strips, sprinkle the chive pieces to garnish. After that, transfer them to a dish to serve immediately.

Mongolia Style Lamb and Leek

Ingredients:

- 250 gm Lamb leg meat,
- Half leek or 3 spring onions,
- 1 Table Spoon finely chopped ginger
- 1 Table Spoon Shaoxing Yellow Rice wine,
- ½ Tea Spoon dark soy sauce,
- ½ Tea Spoon salt
- ½ Tea Spoon sugar
- 1 Tea Spoon freshly ground cumin;
- ½ Tea Spoon chilli powder
- 1 Table Spoon vegetable oil.

Cooking Method:

1. Slice the lamb leg meat into thin pieces,
2. Mix the yellow rice wine, soy sauce, salt, sugar and ginger, and then marinate the lamb pieces in it. (For best result, to marinate it for 1 hour).
3. Slice the leek to about 2 cm (0.8 inches) diagonal shape.
4. Heat up a wok with 1 Table Spoon veg oil,
5. When the oil is very hot, putthe lamb in to stir fry for 2 minutes until the lamb is cooked well and still tender,
6. Add leek or spring onions in toss to mix everything well. After that add ground cumin and chilli, toss a few times to mix everything well.
7. Transfer them in a plate to serve immediately.

RICE AND NOODLES

Steamed Rice

Chinese style rice is traditionally cooked by steaming method. Whereas in the modern era, Chinese style rice is generally cooked in a rice cooker. If you really like fluffy and soft rice, it is worth getting a rice cooker. You can prepare the rice, and then turn the cooker on, you will be able to enjoy some freshly cooked rice at your desired time. If you are not sure, you can try simply steamed rice before getting a rice cooker. Use the method below, you will be able to cook some delicious, fluffy and soft rice.

Ingredients:

- 2 cups of short grain rice,
- 2 cups of cold water.

The ratio is 1:1, 1 cup of rice to 1 cup of water. Follow this ratio, you can adjust the rice you want to cook.

Cooking Method:

1. Wash the rice for a few times,
2. Put the rice in a heat-proof container,
3. Add the water to the rice.
4. Put them in a steamer on high heat to steam for 40 minutes.
5. Once it is cooked, put it in a bowl to enjoy with the dishes you cooked.

Stir-fried Rice with Egg

Ingredients listed are for 2 people

- 2 cups of cooked rice,
- 1 egg,
- 1 spring onion,
- A few drops of vegetable oil,

Cooking Method

1. Slice the spring onion into small pieces,
2. Beaten the egg in a bowl,
3. Heat up a wok with 1 TBSP vegetable oil. When the oil is hot, pour the beaten egg in, and then quickly break the egg into pieces, after that, put the scrambled egg aside to use later.
4. Put Spring onion pieces in the wok, and then, rice, stir fry them together until the rice is hot, approx. 5 minutes, add scrambled egg in to mix well.
5. Transfer the rice to a dish to serve immediately.

Stir-fried Rice with Chicken

Ingredients:

- 2 cups of cooked rice,
- ½ chicken breast,
- 2 spring onions
- 5 Chinese wild mushrooms or Chestnut mushrooms

- 5 French beans
- 2 TSP light soy sauce
- A small bunch of chives. Chopping to fine pieces, approx. 1 TBSP.

Cooking method

1. Slice the chicken breast to approx. 0.5 cm cubes.
2. Slice the spring onion into fine pieces.
3. Slice the mushrooms into fine pieces.
4. Slice the French beans to 0.5 cm length pieces.
5. Heat up a wok with a few drops of vegetable oil in. When the oil is semi-hot, put the spring onion in, stir fry for a few seconds until smell the fragrance. Put the chicken pieces in to cook for 2 – 3 minutes, and then add the French beans, keep stir frying for another minute, add mushroom pieces in. Stir-frying everything in the wok for 1 minute, add soy sauce in and then mix everything in the wok well. In the end, add rice in, keep stir-frying for 2-3 minutes until rice is warmed up thoroughly. Sprinkle chive pieces on the top, and then transfer them to a dish to serve.

Stir-fried Rice Yangzhou Style

Ingredients listed are for 2 people

- 2 cups of cooked rice;
- 1 piece of cooked Cantonese Roast pork, approx. 50 gm.
- 5 raw king prawns,
- ¼ cup of garden peas, or an equivalent quantity of mangetout;
- ¼ cup of sweet corn,
- ¼ cup of finely chopped carrot.
- 1 egg,
- 1 spring onion,
- 1 TSP (tea spoon) Shao Xing rice wine.
- 1 TBSP (table spoon) fine sliced chive for garnish (optional)

Cooking method

1. Slice the back of king prawns to take the black line out if there is any. Cut each king prawn to 3 or 4 pieces, and then, marinate the king prawns in a tea spoon Shao Xing rice wine and a pinch of salt.
2. Slice the Cantonese roast pork to approx. 5mm X 5mm cubes.
3. Beating up 1 egg in a small mixing bowl. Heat up a wok with 1 TBSP vegetable oil. When the oil is hot, pour the beaten egg in to cook scrambled eggs, after that, put the egg aside to use later.
4. Heat up a little oil in the wok to cook king prawns. Once King Prawns are cooked, put them in a bowl to use later.
5. Heat up a little oil, when it is medium hot, add spring onion, carrots, garden peas or mangetout, sweet corn and Cantonese Roast Pork pieces in, sauté for a few times until smell the fragrant smell, and then, add rice and a pinch of salt, turn the heat down to cook it genteelly. Keep mixing everything in the wok for about 10 minutes or until rice is cooked thoroughly hot.
6. Add cooked egg and king prawns, stir fry everything to mix them well. (Garnish with finely chopped chive pieces that are optional) and then transfer them to a dish to serve immediately.

Pineapple Rice

Ingredients:

- 1 Large pineapple,
- 2 Small bowls of steamed rice (or enough for 2 people),
- 3 – 4 Raw King prawns,
- 1 Spring onion,

Ingredients for marinating chicken:

- 1 Table Spoon light soy sauce,
- 2 Table Spoon clear honey,
- 1 Tea Spoon Chinese 5 Spices,

- 50 gm chicken breast marinated for a minimum 4 hours,
- 50 gm Char Siu pork, sliced to small pieces,
- A handful of garden peas, (or half green pepper)
- Half red colour pepper,
- 1 egg,

- 1 Table Spoon Yellow Rice Wine.
- Mix them all together in a mixing bowl.

Cooking method:

1. Cut the top pineapple off with a little bit of pineapple on it,
2. Dig the pineapple meat out by a Pineapple corer, small knife and or your preferred tool,
3. Split king prawns into halves sprinkle a pinch of salt and yellow rice wine to marinate prawns,
4. Slice pineapple into small dices, approx. 0.5cm X 0.5cm X 0.5cm or (0.2" X 0.2" X 0.2")
5. Slice red pepper into a square shape, about a similar size with pineapple.
6. Slice chicken into small dices, slightly bigger than pineapple pieces. And then marinate the chicken in the marinade.
7. Slice spring onion into small pieces,
8. Crack and beat the egg, heat up a wok with a few drops of vegetable oil to fry the egg first. Once it is cooked, put it aside to use later.
9. Heat up a few drops of oil in a wok, when it is hot, put marinated chicken in to toss for a few minutes or until chicken is cooked. Put it aside to use later.
10. Heat up a few drops of vegetable oil in the wok once more, when it is getting hot, add spring onion pieces in, follow by king prawns, and then, chicken, Char Siu pork stir fry for a couple of minutes, and then add pineapple pieces, peas, pepper and rice. Adding 2 Table Spoon marinade, to stir fry everything well, in the end, put a fried egg in to stir fry everything together. Transferring the rice into a pineapple. Put the pineapple top on, serve immediately.

Dandan Noodles

Ingredients:

- 300 gm lean pork leg meat;
- 200 gm Preserved mustard green;
- 1 star anise;
- 150 gm egg noodles (spaghetti is good);
- 2 Tea Spoon dark soy sauce;
- Chilli paste to your taste;
- 1 Tea Spoon salt;

- Some ground Sichuan Huajiao;
- 1 Table Spoon sesame seed paste;
- 1 Table Spoon light soy sauce;
- 1 Table Spoon dark rice vinegar
- 1 Spring onion finely sliced;
- 1 Table Spoon crushed chilli peanuts;
- Some cooking oil.

Cooking method:

1. Soak the mustard green in warm water for half an hour to remove some salt.
2. Chop the pork leg meat to small pieces like mince, and then, marinate it with Sichuan Huajiao;
3. Slice the mustard green to fine piece to match with the pork;
4. Heat up a wok with some cooking oil. When the wok is hot, put the star anise in sauté to bring the fragrance out, and then, take the star anise out, add pork into cook for 10 minutes or until the pork is cooked. Add some dark soy sauce in, chilli paste and some salt, toss to mix them well. After that, add the mustard green in, toss to mix everything well. Transfer them to a bowl to use later.
5. Heat up a sauce pan with some water to boil noodles. When the water is boiling, put some noodles in boiling for 10 minutes or the following the instruction on the package.
6. In a serving bowl, mix the dark rice vinegar, light soy sauce, sesame seed paste, some water from boiling paste together. Transfer some noodles out in the serving bowl, put some cooked pork on the top of noodles, sprinkle some spring onion and crushed chilli peanuts around. Now, the noodle is ready to consume. If you prefer spicy tastes, you can add some chilli oil to the noodles too.

Stir-fried Noodles with Seasonal Vegetables

Ingredients:

- Approx. 200 gm ready to use noodles,
- 1 Pok Choi,
- 100 gm mushroom,
- 75 gm baby corn,
- ½ TSP (tea spoon) salt,

- 1 Garlic Clove,
- 1 spring onion,
- 1 DSP (dish spoon) dark soy sauce
- 1 TBSP (table spoon) light soy sauce
- A few drops of vegetable oil.

Cooking Method,

1. Slice the Pok Choi to strips, approx. 0.5cm X 0.5Cm X 5cm long.
2. Slice mushroom into pieces.
3. Slice the baby corn to approx. 1.5cm length pieces.
4. Slice the spring onion to small pieces, approx. 1cm length.
5. Chop the garlic into fine pieces.
6. Heat up a few drops of vegetable oil in a wok on high heat. When oil is hot, put the spring onion pieces in saute to bring out the fragrance, and then, add the vegetables in stir fry for a couple of minutes, add the dark soy sauce and light soy sauce in, toss to mix everything well, and then, add the noodles in, pouring approx. ¼ cup of cold water a round the wall of the wok put the lid on to cook for 3-4 minutes, remove the lid, add the minced garlic, mix everything well, and then transfer them to a dish to serve immediately.

Stir-fried Noodles with Prawns, Chicken and Vegetables

Ingredients:

- Approx. 200 gm ready to use noodles,
- 30gm Mangetout,
- 50gm baby corn,
- 2 spring onion,
- 2 Chestnut mushrooms,
- 5 raw king prawns,
- ½ piece of chicken breast,

- 1 TBSP (table spoon) Shao Xing Rice wine
- ½ TSP (tea spoon) salt,
- 1 Garlic Clove,
- 1 DSP (dish spoon) dark soy sauce
- 1 TBSP (table spoon) light soy sauce
- A few drops of vegetable oil.

Cooking Method,

1. Slice the spring onion to some trips.
2. Slice the chicken breast to approx. 0.5cm X 0.5cm X 5cm long stips,
3. Slice mushroom into slices,
4. Chop the garlic into fine pieces.
5. Heat up a wok on high heat. When the wok is hot, pour approx. 1 table spoon vegetable oil in, and then, put the chicken pieces into cook for about 5 minutes or until they look pale. Add the king prawns into cook for a couple of minutes or until the king prawns become pink colour, put them in a dish to use later.
6. Heat up a few drops of vegetable oil in a wok. When oil is hot, put the spring onion strips in toss to bring out the fragrance, and then, add the other vegetables in to stir fry for a couple of minutes, add the dark soy sauce and light soy sauce in, toss to mix everything well, and then, add the noodles in, pouring approx. ¼ cup of cold water around the wall of the wok put the lid on to cook for 3-4 minutes, remove the lid, add the minced garlic, the cooked chicken breast and the king prawns in, toss to mix everything well, and then transfer them to a dish to serve immediately.

TRADITIONAL CHINESE DISHES

Baozi 包子 – Steamed Pork Buns

Step 1, forming a dough.

Ingredients of forming the dough:

- 150 Strong white bread flour; plus extra for dusting
- 1/2 Tea Spoon baking powder;
- 5 gm sugar;
- 2 gm salt;
- 7 gm oil;
- 1 sachet yeast or 7 gm yeast;
- 85 ml lukewarm water;
- A few drops of lemon juice.

Cooking Method:

1. In a measuring jug, mixing the sugar, yeast and 85 ml lukewarm water together. Wait for 10 minutes before use.
2. Mix the flour, baking powder, and salt together in a mixing bowl.
3. Before pouring the liquid in the mixed flour, add the oil and a few drops of lemon juice.
4. Pouring the liquid mixture to the flour slowly while mixing them together with a pair of chopsticks or a preferred tool.
5. Once they are mixed, form them into a soft dough. And then keep kneading the dough for 10 minutes. After that, cover the dough in the mixing bowl to rest.

Step 2, making Bao Zi filling.

Ingredients for the Bao Zi filling:

- 100 gm pork mince;
- 2 spring onion finely chopped;
- 2 big slices of ginger to finely chopped, (approx 1 Table Spoon).
- 30 ml chicken stock; or 1 Tea Spoon chicken flavour mixed with 30 ml hot water;
- 1 Table Spoon sesame seed oil;
- 1 Table Spoon light soy sauce;
- ½ - 1 Tea Spoon salt adjust to suit your taste;

Cooking Method:

1. Place the pork mince in a mixing bowl, add the spring onion, ginger, chicken stock, sesame seed oil, light soy sauce in to mix them together very well until they become a paste looking mixture. Cover the mixture up with some cling film, and then put it in the fridge to rest for 1 hour.

Step 3, making Bao Zi.

Cooking Method:

1. Divide the dough into the smaller potion, roll the dough to a long sausage shape, and then separate it to individual balls. Dust the balls with dry flour. Flat each ball with palm, and then flat the pastry further with a rolling pin. Once it becomes a round sheet, put approx. 1 Table Spoon filling in the middle of the dough. To shape a Baozi, use the thumb and a finger to pleat around the edge to close up the bun. When it is done, put it on a dusted board. Repeat the process until finish.

Step 4, steam Bao Zi.

Cooking Method:

1. Heat up a steamer with some water. When water is boiling, top up with some cold water to reduce the temperature to approx. 50 degree C, put freshly wettened cotton or muslin cloth on a metal rack, arrange Bao Zi on the rack with some space in between. Put the lid on, steam for 10 minutes.
2. Turn the heat off, take the Bao Zi out, and put them on a plate to serve immediately.

Char Siu Buns 叉烧包 – Steamed Char Siu buns

There are 4 stages to make Char Siu steamed Pork Buns. First, marinade some pork fillets; second, form a piece of dough; third, making the filling; the last and the most exciting stage is to assemble them together to steam. Ta da, the steamed Char Siu pork buns are ready.

Stage 1, to marinade some pork fillets.

Ingredients:

- Pork fillet 250-300gms;
- 2 Table Spoon dark soy sauce;
- 2 Table Spoon Hoi Sin sauce;
- 1 Table Spoon white sugar or clear honey;
- 1 Table Spoon yellow rice wine.

Cooking Method:

1. Slice the pork fillet into 2 cm thickness pieces.
2. Mix the sauce mentioned above altogether.
3. Marinate the pork for at least 8 hours.
4. Pre-heat the oven to 180 °C fans, 190 °C gas or gas mark 5.
5. Prepare a baking tray with 1cm height cold water, put a wire rack on the top, place marinated pork fillet pieces on the wire rack.
6. Put them in the oven to cook for 7 minutes, and then turn upside down to cook another 7 minutes.
7. They are ready to be consumed.

Stage 2, to form a piece of dough.

Ingredients:

- Strong white bread flour 120 gm;
- Wheat starch 90 gm;
- Dry yeast 1 sachet 7 gm;
- ½ Tea Spoon baking powder;
- 3 Table Spoon white sugar;
- 2 Table Spoon vegetable oil;
- 60 ml milk + 65 ml scalding hot water;
- A few drops of lemon juice.

Cooking Method:

1. Mix 60 ml milk with 65 ml hot water to achieve body temperature, 37 degrees C;
2. Mix the yeast in, also, squeeze a few drops of lemon juice in the bowl.
3. Mix ½ Tea Spoon baking powder in the flour.
4. Add the flour in, mix it with a pair of chopsticks or a spoon to form a very soft piece of dough.
5. Cover the bowl with cling film, put it in a warm place to rise for minimum 1 hour until the dough has doubled in size.
6. Remove the cling film, put 3 Table Spoon white sugar and 2 Table Spoon vegetable oil on the top of the dough.
7. Use one hand to grab the dough repeatedly for 5 minutes until the sugar blended in completely.
8. Add wheat starch in, start to knead the dough for 10 minutes until the dough becomes smooth, elastic and non-sticky.
9. Rest the dough in the bowl and cover the bowl with a piece of cling film for minimum 20 minutes until the dough raises up again.

Stage 3, to make the filling.

Ingredients:

- The cooked pork fillet pieces;
- 3 slices of fresh ginger finely minced to approximately 1 Table Spoon ;
- 2 pieces of fresh spring onion sliced into fine pieces;
- 1 Table Spoon Oyster sauce;
- 1 Table Spoon Hoi Sin Sauce;
- 1 Table Spoon vegetable oil.
- 2 Table Spoon white sugar;
- 1 Table Spoon corn flour + 60 ml cold water

Cooking Method:

1. Slice the pork fillet pieces into 0.5 cm X 0.5 cm cubes.
2. Heat up a wok with 1 Table Spoon vegetable oil.
3. Mix the oyster cause, Hoi Sin sauce, white sugar, corn flour and water together.

4. When the oil is hot, put the ginger mince and spring onion in, sauté for a few times, and then, add the sauce mixture in, keep stirring until the sauce become thick and smooth.
5. Put pork fillet pieces in, toss to cover the pork in the sauce. Put them in a bowl to cool down.

The final stage, to make Char Sui pork buns

Ingredients:

-   The dough made in stage 2;
-   The filling made from stage 3.

Cooking Method:

1. Heat up a steamer with approx. 2 pints of cold tap water.
2. Take the dough out of the bowl. Knead it on a board to form an oval shape. Equalised the dough into 8 small portions.
3. Flatten each small ball with a rolling pin until it becomes a round circle approx. 10cm diameters.
4. Hold the flatten dough piece, on one hand, put approx. 2 Table Spoon filling in the middle of the dough.
5. Snap the edge of the dough to seal it to a ball-shaped parcel. Repeat until all the dough has been made to buns.
6. When the steamer starts to stream, put steamer rack in, with a piece of wettened muslin cloth on the top, and then line up the buns on the rack with plenty of space between each other.
7. Once all the buns are in the steamer, put the lid on, steam on high heat for 10 minutes.
8. Transfer the steamed buns on a plate to enjoy.

Shaomai 烧卖 – Steamed pork dumplings

Ingredients for the dough:

- 2 cup strong bread flour,
- 2 Table Spoon corn flour,
- ½ cup scalding water,
- 1 cup of cold water.
- *extra corn flour for dusting.*

Ingredients for the filling:

- 200 gm pork mince,
- 1 egg,
- 2 spring onion,
- 1 Tea Spoon minced fresh ginger,
- 1 Tea Spoon salt,
- ½ Table Spoon dark soy sauce,
- 1 Tea Spoon chicken flavour

- 1 Celery stem, finely chopped.
- 1 Tea Spoon Yellow Soybean paste,
- 7 King prawns split into a few pieces (optional),
- A few dry Chinese Muer, a type of Chinese mushroom.
- 1 Table Spoon sesame seed oil,

Required cooking utensils are a steamer, a pudding cloth or some baking parchment.

Cooking Method:

1. Mix the flours and water in the ingredients together to make a piece of soft and smooth dough.
2. Heat up a wok with a few drops of veg oil. Beaten the egg and cook it to scrambled egg, and then put it aside to use later.
3. Chop Spring onion and ginger into mince,
4. Mix the pork mince, spring onion, ginger, soy sauce, sesame seed oil, Yellow soybean paste and chicken flavour together. After that, add chopped celery, scrambled eggs, and Muer in.

5. Roll the dough to a long sausage shape, and then separate it to individual balls like golf ball size. Dust the balls with dry corn flour. Flat each ball with palm, and then flat the pastry further with a rolling pin. Once it becomes a round flat shape, put approx. 1 Table Spoon filling in the middle of the dough, crease the sheet by thumb and a finger to form a flower cup, when it is done, put a prawn on the top. Repeat to finish all the dough and the filling.
6. Heat up a steamer with some water. When water is boiling, arrange Shaomai on the rack with some space in between. Put the lid on, steam for 10 minutes.
7. Once they are cooked, serve immediately.

Serving suggestion: It is normally served with some Chinese Dark Vinegar. (Vinegar mixture: 2 Table Spoon vinegar + 1Tea Spoon sugar + 1 Table Spoon hot water + finely chopped ginger and garlic)

Xiajiao 虾饺 – Steamed prawn dumplings

There are 3 stages of cooking prawn dumplings. Firstly, preparing the filling; secondly, forming a dough; the last stage is assembling the dough and filling together.

Ingredients for the filling:

- 150 gm raw king prawns;
- ¼ cup cooked and chopped spinach;
- ½ Tea Spoon salt;
- ½ Tea Spoon sugar;
- 1 Tea Spoon sesame seed oil;
- 1 egg white
- 1 Tea Spoon finely chopped ginger;
- 2 spring onion finely chopped;
- 2 Table Spoon corn starch.

Ingredients for the dough:

- ½ Cup of Wheat Starch,
- ¼ cup of Tapioca Starch,
- ½ cup cold water,
- ½ cup of cold water, put in a sauce pan to heat up until boiling.
- ¼ Tea Spoon salt,

Cooking Method:

Mix the wheat starch, tapioca starch together, and salt together. Add ½ cup cold water in, and mix it well. Heat up another ½ cup of cold water, when it is boiling, pouring the starch mixture in while stirring until it forms a soft dough. Turn the heat off, put the dough on a well-dusted board. (Using wheat starch for dusting.)

Make the filling:

1. Peel and devein the prawns, and then chop the prawns to mince.
2. Separate the egg.
3. Mix the ginger, spring onion and sesame seed oil together. When they are mixed well, add the rest ingredients in including the egg white. Mix everything well, and then, cover the filling with a cling film, put it in a fridge to rest for approx. 1 hour.

Preparing the dipping sauce:

Just mix together the following ingredients.

- 2 Table Spoon dark rice vinegar,
- ¼ Tea Spoon sugar,
- ½ Tea Spoon sesame seed oil,
- 1 Tea Spoon finely chopped garlic, and
- 1 Tea Spoon finely chopped ginger

Cooking utensils required:

A steamer, one or two pieces of Muslin cloth big enough to cover the steamer racks or some bamboo/banana leaves / baking sheets.

Making dumplings:

1. Cut off 1/3 quantity of dough, and roll it to a sausage shape, and then, cut it to 2 cm length pieces.
2. Put one open end upward, and then, flat it with a palm of your hand, after that, flat it further by using a rolling pin until getting a 2mm thick circle.
3. Put approx. 1 Tea Spoon filling in the middle of the pastry, and then, fold it up to seal the edges together. After that fold the top edge to one direction to make wave shape edge. Repeat until finish.
4. Heat up a steamer, when water is boiling, add some cold water, turn the heat down, and then quickly arrange the prawn dumplings on the steaming rack with plenty of space in between. Once it is done, put lid on, and turn the heat up to high again to steam for 5 minutes. Once the dumplings are cooked, take them out of the steamer and serve immediately.

Zhahezi 炸盒子 – Deep fried golden treasure bowls

Ingredients:

- 120 gm plain flour + some for dusting
- 50 ml of cold water
- 50 gm spinach;
- 20 gm Chinese wild mushroom
- 10 gm thin Chinese rice noodles
- 50 gm carrot, finely sliced into rice grain size
- 20 gm coriander finely sliced

- 1 Tea Spoon finely grated ginger root
- 1 ½ Table Spoon light soy sauce
- 1 piece of fermented firm bean curd
- 1 Tea Spoon Chinese Five-Spice
- 1 Table Spoon sesame seed oil
- 1 cup vegetable oil (for cooking)
- 1000 ml cold water (for cooking)

Cooking Method:

1. Mix Plain flour with water. When dry flour becomes crumbs, knead crumbs together to form a dough cover it with cling film, and then, put the dough aside to rest.
2. Soak the thin rice noodles and wild Chinese mushrooms in boiling water for 10 minutes, and then, drain the water, chop the rice noodles and wild mushrooms into small pieces.
3. Boiling some water in a sauce pan, when water is boiling, put spinach in, quickly take it out and drain water, wait for spinach to cool down. When it is cool, squeeze all the water out of spinach. And then slice the spinach into small pieces.
4. Chop the ginger to mince. Slice coriander into tiny pieces.
5. Put the spinach, wild mushroom, carrot, coriander, thin rice noodles and ginger in a mixing bowl. And then, add soy sauce, fermented firm bean curd, Chinese Five-Spice, sesame seed oil. Mix them together well. (Now the filling is ready to use)

To make dumplings:

1. Remove the cling film from the dough and knead it. Roll half of the dough to a sausage shape, and then measure with your fingers to divide the doughs in an equal portion of about 2 cm diameter X 2 cm height cubes and 1 cm diameter X 1cm height small pieces. Dusting some dry flour over them, roll them into balls with the palm of one hand. Press each one flat with the palm of one hand. Flat each piece to paper thin with a rolling pin. Start from the edge push toward the centre. So that the edge is thinner than the centre.

2. Put some filling in the middle of the big pastry, cover the top with a small piece of pasty. seal the edge well by pinching with your thumb and a finger. The edge must be sealed perfectly, otherwise, when cooking in water, the filling will leak out. Once that is done, put this dumpling on a dusted board.

3. Repeat the process until finish.

4. Heat up a sauce pan with plenty of water. When water is boiling, put the Treasure Bowls in. Genteelly stir the water once or twice to make sure the Treasure Bowl are not stuck together. And then, put the lid on. When it is boiling, genteelly stir the water again and keep boiling without the lid for 2-3 minutes until the Treasure Bowls are aired up. Take them out of the sauce pan and keep them separated in a plate to cool down.

5. Heat up a frying pan with a cup of vegetable oil. When the oil is hot, start to fry the cold Treasure Bowls. When the Treasure Bowls are a golden colour, take them out and put them in a dish to serve immediately.

Crispy Golden Treasure Bowls go nicely with Chinese Vinegar (dark rice vinegar).

Making the dipping sauce:

Mix, ¼ cup of dark rice vinegar, ½ Tea Spoon sugar, 1 Tea Spoon sesame seed oil,1 Tea Spoon chilli oil together.

GRILLED DUMPLINGS 锅贴

Pork mince and celery grilled dumplings

Ingredient for making the dough

- 150 gm strong white bread flour + some for dusting
- 75 ml of cold water

Ingredient for making the filling

- 150 gm pork mince
- 50 gm freshly and finely chopped celery (about 2 celery sticks)
- 2 pieces of fresh ginger finely chopped,
- 1 egg,
- 1 spring onion finely chopped,

- 1 TSP chicken flavour powder,
- 1 TBSP light soy sauce
- 1 TBSP sesame seed oil,
- 2 TBSP vegetable oil,
- 1/2 - 1 TSP salt,
- 200 ml of cold water (for cooking).

Cooking Method

1. Mix Plain flour + a pinch salt with 60 ml water, if it is hard, add a little more water. When dry flour becomes crumbs, knead them together, and then, cover the dough with cling film and put it aside to rest.
2. Heat up a wok with a little bit of oil to cook the egg to scrambled eggs.
3. Mix the pork mince with other ingredients together until mixed really well, and then add finely chopped celery and mix everything well.
4. Remove the cling film from the dough, and knead it. Roll half of the dough to a sausage shape, and then measure with your fingers to separate it to small pieces about 2 cm diameter X 2 cm height (0.7" diameter X 0.7" height) cubes. Dust some dry flour over them, roll them into balls with the palm of your hand and then press them flat. After that, using a rolling pin to flatten the dough into a thin sheet, approx. 1-2 mm thick (edge is thinner than the centre).
5. Put some filling in the middle, fold the dough sheet from one side to another, and then, seal the edge well by pinching it with thumb and a finger. Once that is done, put the dumpling on a dusted board.

6. Repeat the process until finish.
7. Heat up a fry-pan on high heat, pour 1 TBSP vegetable oil in the pan. Line up dumplings in the fry-pan with a little gap between each other. When it is very hot, pour some water in the fry-pan, and then put the lid on. Wait until the water is almost run out, removed the lid, drizzling 1 TBSP vegetable oil over the dumplings, turn the heat down a bit. Cook for 1 – 2 minutes until you can hear the sizzling sound. Transfer the dumplings to a dish to serve immediately.

Dumplings go nicely with Chinese Vinegar (dark rice vinegar).

Making the dipping sauce:

Mix, ¼ cup of dark rice vinegar, ½ TSP sugar, 1 TSP sesame seed oil, 1TBSP cold water, ½ TSP finely chopped garlic and ½ TSP finely chopped fresh ginger together.

Beef mince and carrot grilled dumplings

Ingredient for making the dough

- 150 gm plain flour + some for dusting
- 75 ml of cold water

Ingredient for making the filling

- 150 gm beef mince
- 50 gm freshly and finely grated carrot,
- 2 pieces of fresh ginger finely chopped,
- 2 TSP (Tea Spoon) white pepper,
- 1 spring onion finely chopped,
- 1 TSP chicken flavour powder,

- 1 TBSP (Table Spoon) light soy sauce
- 1 TBSP sesame seed oil,
- 2 TBSP vegetable oil,
- 1/2 - 1 TSP salt,
- 200 ml of cold water for cooking.

Cooking Method

1. Mix the Plain flour + a pinch salt with 60 ml water first, if it is hard, add a little more water. When dry flour becomes crumbs, knead them together, and then, cover the dough with cling film and put it aside to rest.

2. Mix the beef mince with other ingredients (ginger, white pepper, spring onion, chicken flavour powder, light soy sauce, sesame seed oil) together until mixed really well, and then add finely grated carrot to mix well. After that, add some salt to suit your taste.

3. Remove the cling film from the dough and knead it genteelly. Roll half of the dough to a sausage shape, and then measure with your fingers to separate it to small pieces about 2 cm diameter X 2 cm height (0.7" diameter X 0.7" height) pieces. Dust some dry flour over them, roll them into balls with a palm of your hand, and then, position one piece with open sides face up and down, press down with your palm to make it flatter. After that, using a rolling pin to flatten the dough into a thin disc, approx. 1-2 mm thick (the edge should be thinner than the centre).

4. Put some filling in the middle, fold the dough disc from one side to another, and seal the edge tightly by pinch it with your thumb and a finger. Once that is done, put the dumpling on a lightly dusted board.
5. Repeat the process until finish.
6. Heat up a fry-pan on high heat, pour 1 TBSP vegetable oil in the pan. Line up dumplings in the fry-pan with some gap in between. When it is very hot, pour some water in the fry-pan, and then put a lid on. Wait until the water is almost running out, removed the lid, drizzling 1 TBSP vegetable oil over the dumplings, turn the heat down a bit. Cook for 1 – 2 minutes until you can hear the sizzling sound. Transfer the dumplings to a dish to serve immediately.

Dumplings go nicely with Chinese Vinegar (dark rice vinegar).

Making the dipping sauce:

Mix, ¼ cup of dark rice vinegar, ½ TSP sugar, 1 TSP sesame seed oil, 1TBSP cold water, ½ TSP finely chopped garlic and ½ TSP finely chopped fresh ginger together.

Vegetable grilled dumplings

Ingredients for making the dough

- 200 gm plain flour + some for dusting
- 100 ml of cold water

Ingredients for making the filling

- 100 gm cabbage
- 100 gm spinach
- 3 garlic cloves minced
- 20 gm thin Chinese rice noodles
- 1 TSP finely grated ginger root

- 1 ½ TBSP light soy sauce
- 2 pieces of fermented soft bean curd
- 1 TBSP sesame seed oil
- 2 TBSP vegetable oil
- 200 ml cold water (for cooking)

Cooking Method

1. Mix Plain flour with water. When dry flour becomes crumbles, knead crumbles together to form a dough, cover it with cling film, and then, put the dough aside to rest.
2. Soak the thin rice noodles in boiling water for 5 minutes, and then, drain the water, chop the rice noodles into small pieces.
3. Boil some water in a sauce pan, when the water is boiling, put the spinach and the cabbage in, quickly drain water, wait for the spinach to cool down. When it is cool, squeeze all the water out of the spinach and the cabbage. And then, slice the spinach and the cabbage into small pieces.
4. Chop ginger to very fine pieces like minced ginger.
5. Mix soy sauce, sesame seed oil and fermented firm bean curd together, and then add spinach, cabbage and thin rice noodles. Mix them well. (Now, the dumpling filling is ready to use.)

Grilled dumplings 锅贴

To make dumplings:

1. Remove the cling film from the dough and knead it. Roll half of the dough to a sausage shape, and then measure with your fingers to divided it to small pieces about 2 cm diameter X 2 cm height (0.7" diameter X 0.7" height) cubes. Dusting some dry flour over them, roll them into balls with the palm of one hand. Press each one flat with the palm of the hand. Flat each piece to paper thin with a rolling pin. Start from the edge push toward the centre. So that the edge is thinner than the centre.
2. Put some filling in the middle, fold pastry from one edge to another, and seal the edge well by pinch with your thumb and a finger. Once that is done, put this dumpling on a dusted board.
3. Repeat the process until finish.
4. Heat up a frying pan on high heat, sprinkle 1 TBSP vegetable oil over the frying pan. Line up dumplings in the frying pan with a little gap between each other. When it is very hot, pouring water in the frying pan, and then put the lid on. Wait until the water is almost finished, removed the lid, sprinkle 1 TBSP vegetable oil over the dumplings, turn the heat down a bit. Cook for 1 – 2 minutes until you can hear a sizzling sound. Put the dumplings in a dish to serve.

Dumplings go nicely with Chinese Vinegar (dark rice vinegar).

Making the dipping sauce: Mix, a ¼ cup of dark rice vinegar, ½ TSP sugar, 1 TSP sesame seed oil, 1 TSP chilli oil.

Won Ton Soup 云吞汤

Ingredients:

- 50 gm plain flour + some for dusting
- 30 gm Pork mince
- 2-3 King Prawns
- 2 mini pork ribs
- Some Goji berries, approx. a hand full.
- ½ Tea Spoon finely grated ginger root + 2 pieces 2mm thick.
- 2 spring onion, 1 finely chopped, 1 sliced into big pieces, approx. 4 cm long.

- 1 Star Anise
- 1 Tea Spoon light soy sauce
- 1 Tea Spoon chicken flavour powder
- 2 egg
- ½ Tea Spoon salt + a pinch
- 1 Tea Spoon sesame seed oil
- 1 Table Spoon shredded dry seaweed
- 1 Table Spoon finely chopped coriander / or chive pieces to garnish optional.

Cooking Method:

1. Soak the ribs in some cold water for 1 hour if you can. Heat up some water in a sauce pan, while water is cold, put ribs in to boil. When it is boiling, remove the foam on the top, add, the ginger pieces, spring onion, Star Anise and Goji Berries in. Turn the heat down to simmer for 1 hour.
2. Mixing the plain flour, an egg white, a pinch of salt, and some cold tap water (approx. 20ml) together. Once it is done, rest for a few minutes, and then, knead it until the dough is smooth.
3. Peel the king prawns and slices each one to 3 or 4 pieces.
4. Mix pork mince, ginger pieces, spring onion, 1 Tea Spoon light soy sauce, ½ Tea Spoon sesame seed oil and chicken flavour powder in a mixing bowl. When everything is mixed well, add king prawns in, mix everything well together.
5. Dust some dry flour on a board or a surface, and then roll the dough to a sausage shape (approx. 2 cm diameter); separate them into small pieces (approx. 2 cm length). Flat each piece by pressing down with the palm of your hand, and then roll it further with a rolling pin until it is approx. 1-2 mm thick.

6. Put some filling in the middle, and then fold it up and seal the edge, stick 2 ends together. Then, a Won Ton is made. Repeat the process until finish.

7. Remove all the bits from the broth. Heat it up again. When it is boiling, put the Won Tons in; stir genteelly around the wall of the sauce pan for a few times. Put the lid on wait until the broth is boiling. While waiting, chop the garnish herbs into small pieces. When broth is boiling, genteelly stirring around the wall of sauce pan again with a spatula. Sprinkle the dry seaweed pieces in the soup; add a pinch of salt; beating an egg in a bowl, and then pouring the beaten egg swirly around from the centre. In the end, sprinkle a few drops of sesame seed oil and some coriander pieces to garnish (optional). Transferring the soup in a bowl to serve immediately.

Su Chun Juan 素春卷

Ingredients

- Approx. 5 sheets of Spring Roll Wrappers (approx. 24 cm X 24 cm),
- 1 Carrot, est. 80 gm;
- 40 gm Cabbage;
- 60 gm bean sprouts;
- A few Chinese wild mushrooms;
- 4 gm or 1 TBSP finely chopped coriander;
- 1 Spring Onion;
- 20 gm Dry Thin Rice Noodles;

- 1 piece of fresh ginger.
- 2 pieces of soft bean curd;
- 1 TSP Chinese Five spices;
- 1 TBSP Light Soy Sauce;
- 1 TSP sugar;
- 1 TSP plain flour + 1 TSP cold water, mix them to paste.
- A Few drops of sesame seed oil,
- 2 cups of vegetable oil.

Cooking Method;

1. Soak Rice noodle in scalding water for 10 – 15 minutes, and then drain the water, leave the rice noodles aside to use later;
2. Shred carrot, cabbage, mushroom to thin strips;
3. Chop the coriander, spring onion, and ginger into fine pieces;
4. Drain water from soaked rice noodles and then slice them into 1" or 2.5 cm length.
5. In a small mixing bowl, mix soft bean curd, Five Spices, light soy sauce, sesame seed oil and sugar together.
6. Put bean sprout, carrot, cabbage, mushroom, soaked rice noodle, coriander, spring onion and ginger in a container. And then, add the mixed sauce in, mix everything well.
7. Spread a spring roll sheet out on a flat surface; put approx. 2 TBSP quantity of the vegetable mixture in the lower centre, towards one corner. Roll the corner up, and then, fold right side and left the side of the roll. Roll it up like a parcel, fasten the roll with a little bit of flour paste. Put it aside. Repeat the process until finish all the fillings.
8. Heat up the vegetable oil in a sauce pan or a wok. When the oil is semi-hot, put spring rolls in. Frying for approx. 10 minutes or until spring rolls look golden colour.
9. Put them on a few pieces of kitchen towel to drain oil a bit, and then transfer them on a plate to serve immediately.

QUESTIONS

Why Chinese food is so popular globally?

Chinese food is very well known globally. You can find Chinese restaurants in almost every country. The popular dishes are Sweet and Sour Chicken, Chicken and Cashew nuts in Yellow Bean Sauce, Chicken in Black Bean Sauce, Stir Fried Noodles and egg fried rice, and many, many more.

The main reasons for Chinese food to be so popular are the tastes, nutrition, and quick to cook. There are so many different styles of Chinese dishes, whatever the taste you like; you will definitely find a favourite dish. Most Chinese dishes use fresh ingredients, plus, every dish contains a few different vegetables with meat to make the dish with rainbow colours, that encourages each ingredient to release the maximum amount of nutrition to the dish. Furthermore, cooking methods also play an important part in creating desired dishes. Here, in this book, I will share the cooking methods commonly used to cook Chinese dishes that can ensure the food is cooked quickly and preserve the maximum nutrition.

Geographically, China is an enormous country. It has over 9.5 million square kilometres in area. The climate is very different from the South to the North, from the West to the East. Each region's nature condition encourages its characteristic food to grow. 5000 years ago, transportation was limited; people could only use the available local produces to create nutritious and tasty dishes. A typical example is that the Beijing cave men started to cook food over an open fire because they found meat tasted more delicious after cooking. Since then, Chinese Food culture has never stopped developing.

People all say that "Chinese food is really healthy, most Chinese people are slim." As a matter of fact, Chinese food promotes healthy eating and balanced dieting philosophy. The combination of meat and vegetable in a dish is always balanced. On the other hand, Chinese dishes should be colourful. Not only for the good presentation, but also for maximum nutritious release.

Chinese people believed that balanced dieting would maintain good health. The theories about how to prepare healthy and nutritious balanced dishes, and what types of food should be consumed in the relevant seasons studied since Confucius time (Confucius was born in 551BC). Generally, green vegetables are count as Ying phase, and meat, especially red meat count as Yang phase. Therefore, every Chinese dish must have a balanced quantity of Ying and Yang characters to achieve a healthy foundation. In winter, people in the north of China consume more slow stew dishes and soup to obtain heat source and gentle nutritious required for their bodies. In summer, people eat more green vegetable and salad to neutralize the temperatures between outside and inside of the body. Everybody knows Si Chuan cuisine has hot and spicy characters. Why? Because in Si Chuan region, the climate is wet and damp all year round. Chilli has the special function of pushing exceed damp air out of the body. For this purpose, Si Chuan people eat a considerable amount of chillies every day prevent joint pain.

The last but not the least is that Chinese Food is so quick to cook that suits our modern life style. Most of Chinese food can be cooked ready in 5 or 10 minutes, for example, Stir Fried rice, Chao Mian, and many other stir-fried dishes. Imagine, you come home after work, you really want something delicious, healthy and quick to prepare. If you slice some vegetables and meat, stir fry them in a wok with your favourite sauces. In half an hour, you will be able to sit down enjoy freshly cooked Chinese food for your dinner.

After all, the biggest secret of creating delicious Chinese food is knowing your ingredients. That is the knowledge I am going to share with you.

THE BASIC INGREDIENTS OF COOKING A CHINESE DISH

The very basic flavouring ingredients used in any cooking are salt and oil. No matter what cuisine you cook, you can't leave these two. Salt is the same everywhere. You can use sea salt, table salt or any type of salt you like. Whereas oil, depends on which regions, there are a different preference. Now, let's have a look at the types of oil used in Chinese cooking.

Oil

In Chinese cooking, unsaturated vegetable oil, ground nuts oil, soybean oil, and seed oil are widely used. For example, vegetable oil is healthier and economic to cook deep fry dishes because the cost of vegetable oil is cheaper than ground nuts oil. Vegetable oil is suitable for cooking every dish as it is flavourless, whereas, some chefs prefer to use ground nuts oil to give dishes a nutty flavour.

Another type of oil is also widely used in Chinese cooking that is sesame seed oil. In China, the traditional method of making sesame seed oil is to toast sesame seeds first until strong sesame seed smell is released. And then, the seeds will be pressed to obtain the oil. The colour of sesame seed oil is dark brown. It has a very strong sesame seed smell.

Whereas in Western countries, some sesame seed oil is pressed from raw seed. It is also called the cold press. This type of oil has a pale colour and little smell of sesame seeds.

Pastes, they are typical Chinese Cooking sauces. Depends on the raw materials from each region, different pastes taste differently. However, they are produced in a similar process.

The followings are a few popular fermented pastes that have strong and unique tastes commonly used in Chinese cooking. They are yellow bean paste, Hoisin sauce, black bean paste, Sichuan chilli and bean paste, etc. Yellow bean paste was originally invented in the North of China; Hoisin sauce was started in the South of China. Black bean paste and Sichuan chilli and bean paste was firstly made in Sichuan region where chilli was prosperously grown. Let's have a look at each characteristic closer.

Soy Sauce

The main ingredients in a soy sauce are dried soybean pancake, starch, and wheat flour. Applying with fermenting manufacture method, that is how soy sauce is made. In general, there are 3 types, light, dark and medium soy sauce commonly used in China. Light and dark soy sauce are usually used in the South of China, whereas, the medium soy sauce is widely used in the North of China. The taste of light soy sauce is salty with soy bean's fermenting flavour. That is recommended for adding in a salad. Dark soy sauce tastes less salty comparing with light soy sauce. It contains burnt caramel. So, it tastes sweet too. The dark soy sauce is much thicker than light soy sauce. It looks red-dark brown. As dark soy sauce is a rich and thick type of sauce, it is usually used in marinate and stew meat dishes. Medium soy sauce is a combination of light and dark soy sauce. Not only medium soy sauce has sweet, salty and fermenting soybean taste, but also has a gentle dark brown colour. It looks very similar to black coffee. Medium soy sauce is suitable for use in almost every Chinese dish, from salad dressing, stir-fries to stew etc.

- Light soy sauce tastes savoury
- Light soy sauce looks watery
- Its colour is brown
- It is suitable for making salad dressing and stir fries

- Medium soy sauce tastes savoury
- Medium soy sauce looks much thinner than dark soy sauce
- Its colour is dark brown
- It is suitable for cooking everything

- Dark soy sauce tastes savoury with a hint of sweetness.
- Dark soy sauce looks thick
- Its colour is red-dark brown.
- It is suitable for marinate and stew.

Pastes

The followings are a few popular fermented pastes that have strong and unique tastes commonly used in Chinese cooking. They are yellow bean paste, Hoisin sauce, black bean paste, Sichuan chilli and bean paste, etc. Yellow bean paste was originally invented in the North of China; Hoisin sauce was started in the South of China. Black bean paste and Sichuan chilli and bean paste was firstly made in Sichuan region where chilli was prosperously grown. Let's have a look at each characteristic closer.

Yellow Bean Paste

Yellow bean paste is made from fermenting dried and compressed soy bean pancakes, wheat flour products and salt together. It has strong soybean and savoury tastes. The appearance of this paste is smooth, dark chocolate looking paste. When used in a recipe, it can give a dish rich soybean taste and brown colour. There are two types of Yellow bean paste in the market, one is called sweet yellow bean paste (in Chinese its name is tian mian jian); another is called big yellow bean paste (in Chinese its name is da jiang). The sweet yellow bean paste tastes sweet and savoury. Traditionally, it was made in Tianjin and Shangdong Region. Whereas, big yellow bean paste tastes savoury only. The signature dishes cooked with this pastes are Chicken Cashew Nut and Yellow Bean Sauce, Pork strips and spring onion Tianjin Style. Tianjin style aubergine, etc.

Hoisin Sauce

Hoisin sauce is a paste type of sauce. Its colour is dark red. Its texture is smooth. Originally, it is from the South of China, such as Guangzhou & Hong Kong, etc. Although it is a soybean and wheat starch-based paste. It has added garlic flavour and sugar. It contains a mixed of sweet, savoury and garlicky fragrance tastes. Hoisin sauce is commonly used to glaze meat, or used as a dipping sauce for roast meat. Hoisin sauce also goes well with seafood. For example, when used as a dipping sauce, it served with Cantonese Roast Duck or Roast pork, beef in Mandarin sauce, etc.

Black Bean Paste

Black bean sauce is made from fermenting black bean with salt. During the process, garlic is added too to give a delicious smell. The appearance of black bean paste is black and lumpy. From its name you probably can imagine that its main ingredient is black beans, during the fermenting process, the beans are crashed into pieces to push the flavour out, but not blended to smooth paste. The taste of black bean paste is savoury mixed with a somewhat bitter hint. It is commonly used as a cooking sauce in stir-fry dishes. For example, chicken in black bean sauce, tofu in black bean sauce, etc.

Sichuan Chilli & Bean Paste

The main ingredients in Sichuan chilli & bean paste are board beans, chillies, Sichuan local spice called Sichuan Huajiao, garlic and salt, etc. The paste looks like ground solid red chilli pieces. It has a fiery spicy taste. It is a crucial ingredient in Sichuan cuisine. It can be used in stir fry, salad, marinate, stew, etc. For example, Sichuan fish boiled in water, Return to wok pork, and Yuxiang (fish fragrant) aubergine pot, etc.

Sugar

Sugar is commonly used in Chinese Cooking. There are 2 types of recipes, granulated sugar and rock sugar. Granulated sugar melts quickly. It is used to give a dish a hint of sweet flavour. Rock sugar has a different crystal structure. It is usually used in Hong Shao meat dishes to give the meat a glossy coating.

Granulated sugar colour is white, and its particle is fine.

Rock Sugar looks like crystal rock.

Vinegar

Vinegar is an important ingredient in many Chinese dishes. The commonly used types of vinegar in Chinese cooking are dark rice vinegar and clear rice vinegar. Both of them are made by fermenting rice to obtain acetic acid. Dark rice vinegar has a rich dark brown colour. It also has a sour and sweet taste. Normally, it is used as a dipping sauce when having dumpling. Clear rice vinegar has no colour, it looks like clear water. Clear rice vinegar is usually used to give a dish sour flavour, but not adding any colour to the dish. For example, sweet and sour chicken, lemon chicken, etc.

Yellow Rice Wine

You might be able to imagine from the name that this wine is made from yellow rice. Yellow rice predominantly grew in Shaoxing China. So, it is called Shaoxing Rice wine too. Like Chinese people in other regions brewing alcohol drinks, the local people used this type of rice. The differences between this type of rice wine are the colour and taste. The colour of yellow rice wine is light brown like Whisky colour. And the taste is gentle sour and smooth with berry flavour. In Chinese recipes, it is used for adding fresh fruit flavour, it is also used in the marinade to remove the unpleasant smell from meat and fish. The alcohol content of yellow rice wine is around 15%, so, it can be served as a dinner drink for a meal.

The colour is clear light brown.

The taste is gentle sour.

The smell is like sherry.

Cooking Method

Stir-fry

The commonly known cooking method for Chinese food is "Stir-fry". Stir fry method allows dishes to created quickly. It requires to use high heat. Stir fry method is suitable for cooking most of the Chinese dishes from fresh ingredients.

Steam

You will need a steamer to use this method. This method is suitable for cooking something requires longer cooking time, such as meat and ribs, or cooking buns. Normally, we should start to count cooking time when the steam comes out.

Boiling

This method is usually used to cook meat and something requires a bit longer cooking time. Once the meat is almost cooked, we will use the braising method to give it flavours.

Frying Method

Frying method includes deep fry, shallow fry and water fry. Deep fry requires plenty of oil to cover the ingredients needed to be fried. It requires medium to high heat. Shallow fry uses much less oil. Normally, we fry one side and then turn to another side. Water fry is considered as a method to cook something healthy, crispy and delicious. It uses approx. 1 tablespoon of oil to start with, and then, add some water to cover the food you are cooking on high heat. Once, the water is almost evaporated, sprinkle another tablespoon of oil and turn down the heat to cook a few more minutes to achieve the golden and crispy result. Grilled dumplings have used this method to cook.

Meiru Ludlow

Printed in the United States
By Bookmasters